GOD MUST LIKE TO LAUGH

Written and Illustrated by
Helen Caswell

Abingdon Press
Nashville

GOD MUST LIKE TO LAUGH

Copyright © 1987 by Abingdon Press

Library of Congress Cataloging-in-Publication Data

Caswell, Helen Rayburn.
  God must like to laugh.

  Summary: Speculates in verse on the enjoyment God must have had as he created the wide variety of wonders in the animal world.
  1. God—Juvenile literature. 2. Laughter—Religious aspects—Christianity—Juvenile literature. [1. God. 2. Animals—Religious aspects] I. Title.
BT107.C37 1987   231   87-1362
ISBN 0-687-15188-0 (pbk. : alk. paper)

MANUFACTURED IN HONG KONG

God made the world—the heavens, too—
And night and day, and me and you.

But along with big things like the sun,
God must have had a lot of fun

Attending to each small detail:
The fragile shell upon the snail,

The flowers fitted to the bee,
And little bugs too small to see,

The camels and the kangaroos,
And things you only see in zoos,

The penguin and the platypus,
The monstrous hippopotamus,

The wondrous webs the spiders spin,

The way cats purr, the way dogs grin.

And just because God took a notion,
We have whales spouting in the ocean.

We have the llama and the shrew,
The green bullfrog and peacocks blue,

And snakes and bats and all those others
That only God could love—or mothers.

How would God think up all those things?
The different song that each bird sings,

The cockatoo and crocodile—
I think they must have made God smile.
It must have been the way he played.

And when at last they all were made,
From tiny gnat to tall giraffe,
I wish I could have heard God laugh!

To Ruth Avalon Caswell
whose laughter makes
everyone feel like laughing